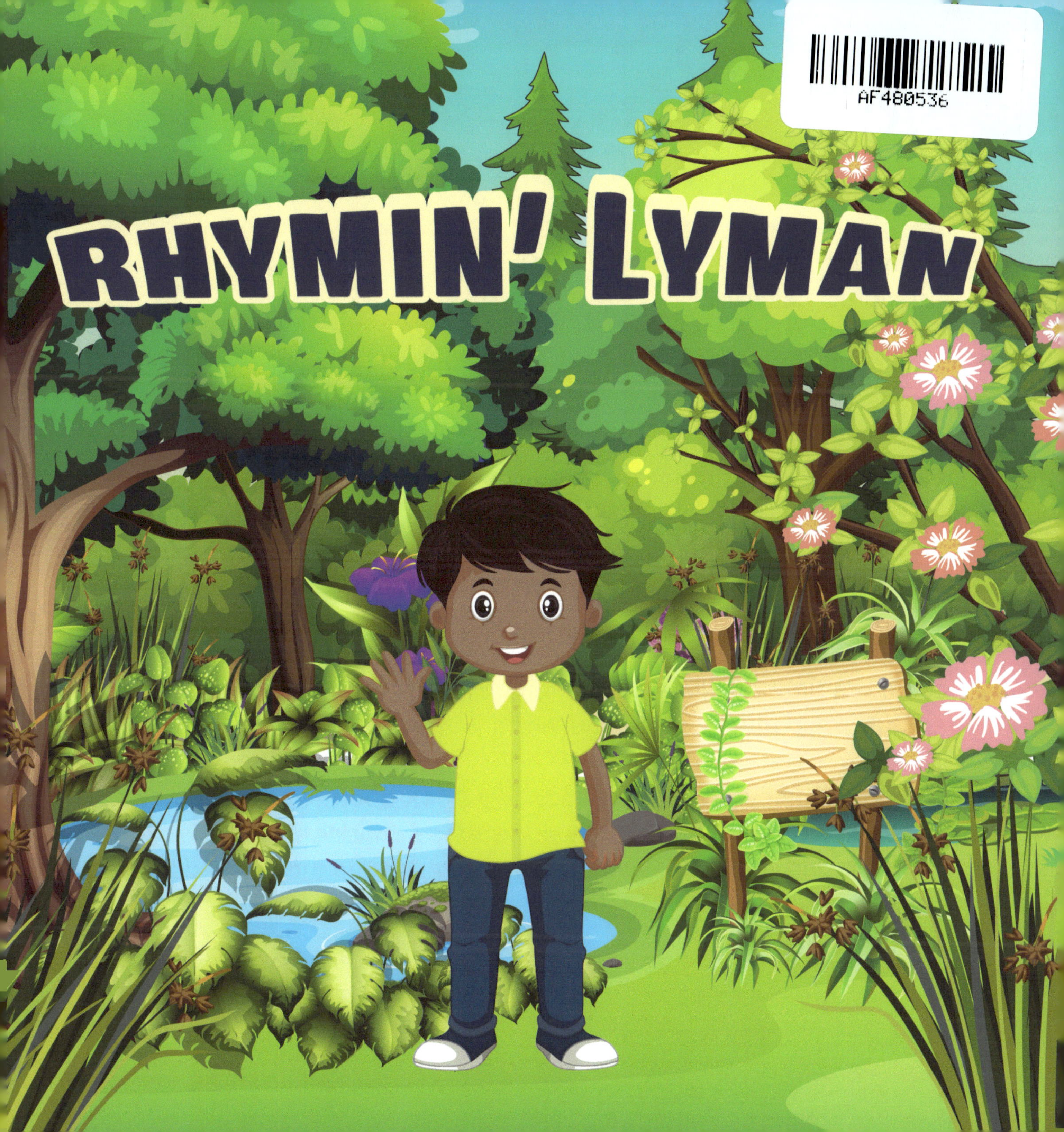
RHYMIN' LYMAN

Story summary: Rhymin' Lyman is a book about a young boy who, like his friend Rhymin' Diamon', teaches children what makes a rhyme and how to figure out whether two or more words do rhyme without fail.

Dedication:

This book is dedicated to
my past and present colleagues
who have been very supportive and excited to hear
about my books and to even invite me
to read them to their classes.

Also,
This series of books is for all the children
out there that have
fallen in love with rhymes like I have.

RHYMIN' LYMAN

My name is Rhymin' Lyman and
I'm here to say, I'm a friend
of Rhymin' Diamon'
so lets rhyme it this way.

This whole book is loaded
with rhymes,
for you to find all the times.

Some are quite easy for you to spot, but others you may find just are not.

Now lets look at how we find,
two or more words of
the rhyming kind.
tell
mood
bell
food
jog
fog

To find two or more words
that rhyme in this way,
you have to listen to what
they really do say.

It doesn't really matter
how they're spelled,
because they will rhyme even
when they're yelled.

The spelling may throw you
for a **loop**,
just like you see in the
rhyming word **soup**.

You need to read them and
listen to their sound,
and a rhyme just surely
may be found.

This description will always work,
so you won't find a single quirk.

To find two or more words that truly do rhyme, you read them all in very good time.

Listen to the *middle*
and *end* of each word,
this is where the rhyme
will be heard.

If the *middle* and *end*
sound the same,
then you have just made
the rhyming game.

This is what I really do mean,
here are some words to
hear what is seen.

Let's take a look at
cook and **book**.
They both have the **"ook"** sound
in the word, so the rhyme
will always be heard.

Cook
Book

Another pair for you to hear is
the words *bee,* and even *three.*
With words this short
it's easy to hear,
the *"long e"* sound is very clear.

Then there's **bird** and **word** we found. These two rhyme because of the "*ird*" sound.
Word

When you find words
that rhyme you will see,
it can be more than two,
maybe even three.

I know there can be four,
or maybe even more?

Now let's look at some like
coat, goat and even a float.
That was three, all saying
the "long o" and also a "t".

How about words like **date,**
straight, and maybe even **eight.**
Here are three that really sound great.
When you read each of them
you will hear the "**long a**" & also a "**t**".

Let's take a look to find
some more,
you will see there's lots of
fun in store.

This time we'll look at words like *two*, *goo*, *new*, *flu*, and even *blue*. When you read them all you will hear the *"oo"*.

Can you find the rhyme to every word,
read them all and the rhyme will be heard.
There may be more than one in the group,
so don't let that throw you for a loop.

jog	cake	frog	fog
fat	tree	met	bat
bar	truck	jar	scar
bird	herd	dock	word
four	boy	score	door
make	cake	steak	leak
lose	news	goose	bruise
great	grate	seat	late
home	foam	come	comb

Then there are words that sound the same,
they surely rhyme because they have
the same name.

do   dew   due

sun   son

lone   loan

none   nun

That was just the tiniest list, but there's still some I've surely missed. Can you think of more to increase your score?
04 00

These rhyming rules do apply to a name,
it's really all just the same. Let's take
look at a name like Stan and you can
see it will rhyme with fan.
How about a girl named Meg surely
that will rhyme with egg.

Now is your time to find your own rhyme.
Try to find one for each word,
or maybe two, or even a third:

plan _______ _______ _______

bee _______ _______ _______

fox _______ _______ _______

soy _______ _______ _______

cat _______ _______ _______

Now can you find all the rhymes
in this book? I bet you can
if you take a good look.

There are many more than
the ones I point out,
that you will see there
can be no doubt.

It's time now to go back to the start, and look on each page to do your part.
Start

Count, count, and count them all, the number surely will not be small.

It's lots of fun to find
the rhyme, just go ahead and
have a good time.

This fun little book is just
the beginning, so now keep
it up and you'll find
you are winning.
Finish